HUMMINGBIRD'S WINGS

retold by Vita Jiménez
illustrated by Jason Parker

CHAPTER 1

✦

A Special Bird

Long ago, there was a Great Spirit. He looked after every animal in the kingdom. One day, he created a tiny bird. The bird was plain looking, but Great Spirit gave her wings that were very special.

The bird could flap her wings faster than any other bird. She could fly backwards or stay in one spot. When she did this, her wings made the most splendid humming sound. That is why Great Spirit named her Hummingbird.

As she got older, Hummingbird looked at the birds around her. Some had red feathers and some had blue feathers. Some even had yellow feathers. At first, this made Hummingbird sad.

"Why do I have such plain feathers?" she said.

The other birds said, "You may be plain, but you make music when you fly!"

This made Hummingbird feel good.

One day, Hummingbird met another bird. They decided to get married. But there was a problem. Hummingbird didn't have money to buy a wedding dress. She was so sad that she stopped flying. This made the other birds sad, too. They missed her humming sound.

"Let's help our friend," said Spider.

"What can we do?" asked the bird with the red feathers.

"Let's all think hard," said Spider. "Together we can come up with a plan."

All the animals nodded. They wanted Hummingbird to be happy. They wanted her to fly and hum again.

CHAPTER 2

Helping Hummingbird

The bird with the red feathers had a good idea. "Hummingbird can use my feathers for a necklace," he said. He plucked off eight feathers and tied them together.

All the birds plucked off
feathers. Blue bird helped
carry them to the tailor.
The tailor could make a
very special gown with
the feathers.

Spider said, "I can spin silk for a delicate veil." Then she helped the tailor with the gown.

Finally, everything was ready! Hummingbird's friends rushed to give her their gifts.

When it was time for the wedding, all the animals gathered around. Honeybee brought honey and nectar. The trees and bushes brought their flowers and fruits. The butterflies fluttered around gaily.

Hummingbird put on her wedding gown, veil, and necklace. She was so happy that she forgot about being sad. She flew around, making the most wonderful humming sound. The Great Spirit's heart was filled with joy.

"Hummingbird, I hope you now see how special you are," he said. "Only you can make music with your wings."

Respond to Reading

Retell

Use your own words to retell *Hummingbird's Wings* in order.

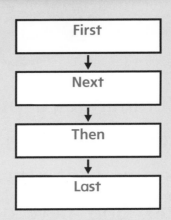

First
↓
Next
↓
Then
↓
Last

Text Evidence

1. What does the bird with the red feathers do to help Hummingbird? Sequence

2. What happens after Hummingbird's friends give her the gifts? Sequence

3. What kind of story is this? How do you know that *Hummingbird's Wings* is a folktale? Genre

Compare Texts
Read to find out more about
hummingbirds.

What Is a Hummingbird?

Hummingbird wings beat very, very fast. Some hummingbirds beat their wings 60 to 80 times a second! This quick movement makes a humming sound. This is why the bird is called a hummingbird.

Hummingbirds

What They Look Like	What They Eat	How They Fly
Hummingbirds are very tiny. They perch and scoot sideways, but they can't walk or hop. They have strong bodies and long wings. Their bills are long, slender, and slightly curved.	Hummingbirds eat nectar. They do not eat seeds like other birds.	Hummingbirds can fly forward, straight up and down, and backwards. They can hover, or appear to stay in one place, while beating their wings quickly.

Make Connections

Look at both selections. What did you learn about hummingbirds?

Text to Text

Focus on Genre

Folktale A folktale is a story based on traditions and customs. Folktales are told orally and often teach lessons.

What to Look for Hummingbird teaches us that we are special just the way we are. The animals talk and act like people. In real life, animals don't do these things.

Your Turn

Make up a story about why a different animal is special. What can it do? Draw a picture and write what makes it special.